Flávia Gonçalves Fernandes

Database in SQL Server Software

Flávia Gonçalves Fernandes

Database in SQL Server Software

Solving Exercises

ScienciaScripts

Imprint

Any brand names and product names mentioned in this book are subject to trademark, brand or patent protection and are trademarks or registered trademarks of their respective holders. The use of brand names, product names, common names, trade names, product descriptions etc. even without a particular marking in this work is in no way to be construed to mean that such names may be regarded as unrestricted in respect of trademark and brand protection legislation and could thus be used by anyone.

Cover image: www.ingimage.com

This book is a translation from the original published under ISBN 978-613-9-63933-5.

Publisher:
Sciencia Scripts
is a trademark of
Dodo Books Indian Ocean Ltd. and OmniScriptum S.R.L publishing group

120 High Road, East Finchley, London, N2 9ED, United Kingdom
Str. Armeneasca 28/1, office 1, Chisinau MD-2012, Republic of Moldova, Europe
Printed at: see last page
ISBN: 978-620-7-71532-9

SUMMARY

CHAPTER 1

DATABASE IN SQL SERVER SOFTWARE: SOLVING EXERCISES

Consider the following database model:

Dept (CodPepto, NomeDepto)

Discipline (CodDepto, NumDisc, NomePisc, CreditosPisc)

        Pepto reference code

PreReq (CodPepto, NumPisc, CodPeptoPreReq, NumPiscPreReq)

      (CodPepto, NumPisc) discipline reference

      (CodPeptoPreReq, NumPiscPreReq) Piscipline reference

Class (YearSem, CodPepto, NumPisc, SiqlaTur, CapacTur)

      (CodPepto, NumPisc) discipline reference

Timetable (AnoSem, CodPepto, NumPisc, SiqlaTur, PiaSem, Horalnicio,

NumHours, CodPred, NumSala)

      (YearSem, CodPepto, NumPisc, SiglaTur) Class reference

      (CodPred, NumSala) referenceSala

Building (CodPred, NamePred)

Room (CodPred, RoomNum, RoomCapacity)

     CodPred reference Building

Teacher (CodProf, NameProf, CodTit, CodPepto)

      CodTit reference Title

      CodPepto reference Professor

ProfClass (YearSem, CodPepto, NumPisc, SiqlaTur, CodProf)

      (YearSem, CodPepto, NumPisc, SiglaTur) Class reference

      CodProf reference Professor

Title (CodTit, NameTit)

Use the script below to insert data into the IMIH database, knowing that the underlined fields are keys. Don't forget to declare the foreign keys.

Create database IMIH

Use IMIH

```sql
create table Depto
(codDepto char(5),
nomeDepto varchar(20),
primary key (codDepto));

insert into Depto
values ('INF01', 'Informática');

insert into Depto
values ('MAT01', 'Matemática');

insert into Depto
values ('ELE01', 'Eletrônica');
```

ADM.Flavia_IMIH - dbo.Depto

	codDepto	nomeDepto
▶	ELE01	Eletrônica
	INF01	Informática
	MAT01	Matemática
✳	NULL	NULL

```sql
create table Disciplina
(codDepto char(5),
numDisc char(5),
nomeDisc varchar(20),
creditosDisc int,
primary key (codDepto, numDisc),
foreign key (codDepto) references Depto);

insert into Disciplina
values ('INF01', 'DIS01', 'Ling Formais', 4);

insert into Disciplina
values ('INF01', 'DIS02', 'Teoria da Comp', 4);

insert into Disciplina
values ('INF01', 'DIS03', 'Programacao I', 8);

insert into Disciplina
values ('MAT01', 'DIS04', 'Cálculo 1', 4);

insert into Disciplina
values ('MAT01', 'DIS01', 'Cálculo 2', 6);
```

ADM.Flavia_IMIH - dbo.Disciplina

	codDepto	numDisc	nomeDisc	creditosDisc
▶	INF01	DIS01	Ling Formais	4
	INF01	DIS02	Teoria da Comp	4
	INF01	DIS03	Programacao I	8
	MAT01	DIS01	Cálculo 2	6
	MAT01	DIS04	Cálculo 1	4
✳	NULL	NULL	NULL	NULL

```sql
create table PreReq
(codDepto char(5),
numDisc char(5),
codDeptoPreReq char(5),
numDiscPreReq char(5),
primary key (codDepto, numDisc, codDeptoPreReq, numDiscPreReq),
foreign key (codDepto, numDisc) references disciplina,
foreign key (codDeptoPreReq, numDiscPreReq) references disciplina);

insert into PreReq
values ('INF01', 'DIS02', 'INF01', 'DIS01');

insert into PreReq
values ('MAT01', 'DIS04', 'MAT01', 'DIS01');

insert into PreReq
values ('INF01', 'DIS03', 'INF01', 'DIS02');
```

ADM.Flavia_IMIH - dbo.PreReq

codDepto	numDisc	codDeptoPreReq	numDiscPreReq
INF01	DIS02	INF01	DIS01
INF01	DIS03	INF01	DIS02
MAT01	DIS04	MAT01	DIS01
NULL	NULL	NULL	NULL

```sql
create table Turma
(anoSem int,
codDepto char(5),
numDisc char(5),
siglaTur char(5),
capacTur int,
primary key (anoSem, codDepto, numDisc, siglaTur),
foreign key (codDepto, numDisc) references Disciplina);

insert into Turma
values (20021, 'INF01', 'DIS01', 'TUR01', 30);

insert into Turma
values (20022, 'INF01', 'DIS01', 'TUR01', 30);

insert into turma
values (20021, 'INF01', 'DIS02', 'TUR02', 30);

insert into Turma
values (20022, 'INF01', 'DIS03', 'TUR01', 200);

insert into Turma
values (20031, 'INF01', 'DIS03', 'TUR02', 30);

insert into Turma
values (20021, 'MAT01', 'DIS01', 'TUR01', 15);

insert into Turma
values (20022, 'INF01', 'DIS03', 'TUR02', 25);
```

	anoSem	codDepto	numDisc	siglaTur	capacTur
▶	20021	INF01	DIS01	TUR01	30
	20021	INF01	DIS02	TUR02	30
	20021	MAT01	DIS01	TUR01	15
	20022	INF01	DIS01	TUR01	30
	20022	INF01	DIS03	TUR01	200
	20022	INF01	DIS03	TUR02	25
	20031	INF01	DIS03	TUR02	30
✳	NULL	NULL	NULL	NULL	NULL

(ADM.Flavia_IMIH – dbo.Turma)

```sql
create table Predio
(codPred int,
nomePred varchar(30),
primary key (codPred));

insert into Predio
values (43423, 'Informática-Aulas');

insert into Predio
values (43421, 'Administração');

insert into Predio
values (43424, 'Laboratórios');
```

	codPred	nomePred
▶	43421	Administração
	43423	Informática-Aulas
	43424	Laboratórios
✳	NULL	NULL

(ADM.Flavia_IMIH – dbo.Predio)

```sql
create table Sala
(codPred int,
numSala int,
capacSala int,
primary key (codPred, numSala),
foreign key(codPred)references Predio);

insert into Sala
values (43423, 101, 30);

insert into Sala
values (43421, 102, 50);

insert into Sala
values (43424, 215, 40);
```

	codPred	numSala	capacSala
▶	43421	102	50
	43423	101	30
	43424	215	40
✳	NULL	NULL	NULL

(ADM.Flavia_IMIH – dbo.Sala)

```sql
create table Horario
(anoSem int,
codDepto char(5),
numDisc char(5),
siglaTur char(5),
diaSem int,
horaInicio char(5),
numHoras int,
codPredio int,
numSala int,
primary key (anoSem, codDepto, numDisc, siglaTur, diaSem, horaInicio),
foreign key (anoSem, codDepto, numDisc, siglaTur) references turma,
foreign key (codPredio, numSala) references sala);

insert into Horario
values (20021, 'INF01', 'DIS01', 'TUR01', 2, '10:30', 60, 43423, 101);

insert into Horario
values (20021, 'INF01', 'DIS02', 'TUR02', 3, '10:30', 60, 43423, 101);

insert into Horario
values (20022, 'INF01', 'DIS03', 'TUR02', 4, '08:30', 45, 43424, 215);

insert into Horario
values (20021, 'INF01', 'DIS01', 'TUR01', 4, '13:30', 60, 43423, 101);
```

ADM.Flavia_IMIH - dbo.Horario

anoSem	codDepto	numDisc	siglaTur	diaSem	horaInicio	numHoras	codPredio	numSala
20021	INF01	DIS01	TUR01	2	10:30	60	43423	101
20021	INF01	DIS01	TUR01	4	13:30	60	43423	101
20021	INF01	DIS02	TUR02	3	10:30	60	43423	101
20022	INF01	DIS03	TUR02	4	08:30	45	43424	215
NULL	NULL	NULL	NULL	NULL	NULL	NULL	NULL	NULL

```sql
create table Titulacao
(codTit int,
nomeTit varchar(20),
primary key (codTit));

insert into Titulacao
values (1, 'Doutor');

insert into Titulacao
values (2, 'Mestre');

insert into Titulacao
values (3, 'Especialista');

insert into Titulacao
values (4, 'Graduado');
```

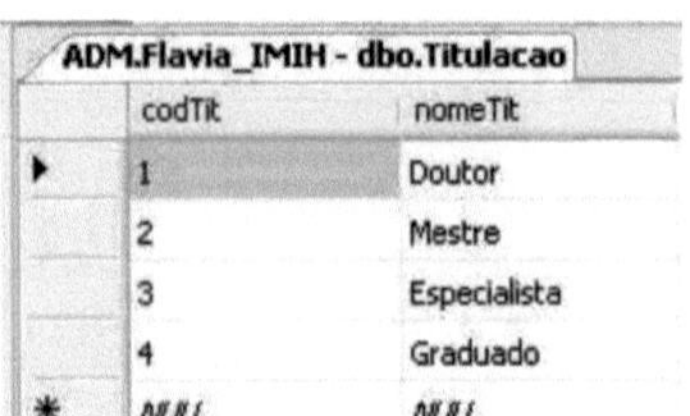

ADM.Flavia_IMIH - dbo.Titulacao

codTit	nomeTit
1	Doutor
2	Mestre
3	Especialista
4	Graduado
NULL	NULL

```sql
create table Professor
(codProf char(5),
nomeProf varchar(50),
codTit int,
codDepto char(5),
primary key (codProf),
foreign key (codTit) references Titulacao,
foreign key (codDepto) references Depto);

insert into Professor
values ('Pro01', 'Antunes', 1, 'INF01');

insert into Professor
values ('Pro02', 'Maria dos Santos', 2, 'INF01');

insert into Professor
values ('Pro03', 'Paulo', 3, 'MAT01');

insert into Professor
values ('Pro04', 'Gabriel', 2, 'MAT01');
```

ADM.Flavia_IMIH – dbo.Professor

codProf	nomeProf	codTit	codDepto
Pro01	Antunes	1	INF01
Pro02	Maria dos Santos	2	INF01
Pro03	Paulo	3	MAT01
Pro04	Gabriel	2	MAT01
NULL	*NULL*	*NULL*	*NULL*

```sql
create table ProfTurma
(anoSem int,
codDepto char(5),
numDisc char(5),
siglaTur char(5),
codProf char(5),
primary key (anoSem, codDepto, numDisc, siglaTur, codProf),
foreign key (anoSem, codDepto, numDisc, siglaTur) references Turma
foreign key (codProf) references Professor);

insert into ProfTurma
values (20021, 'INF01', 'DIS01', 'TUR01', 'Pro01');

insert into ProfTurma
values (20022, 'INF01', 'DIS01', 'TUR01', 'Pro01');

insert into ProfTurma
values (20021, 'INF01', 'DIS02', 'TUR02', 'Pro02');

insert into ProfTurma
values (20021, 'MAT01', 'DIS01', 'TUR01', 'Pro03');

insert into ProfTurma
values (20021, 'MAT01', 'DIS01', 'TUR01', 'Pro02');
```

ADM.Flavia_IM... dbo.ProfTurma				
anoSem	codDepto	numDisc	siglaTur	codProf
20021	INF01	DIS01	TUR01	Pro01
20021	INF01	DIS02	TUR02	Pro02
20021	MAT01	DIS01	TUR01	Pro02
20021	MAT01	DIS01	TUR01	Pro03
20022	INF01	DIS01	TUR01	Pro01
NULL	NULL	NULL	NULL	NULL

CHAPTER 2

List 01

1. Obtain all the teachers' data.

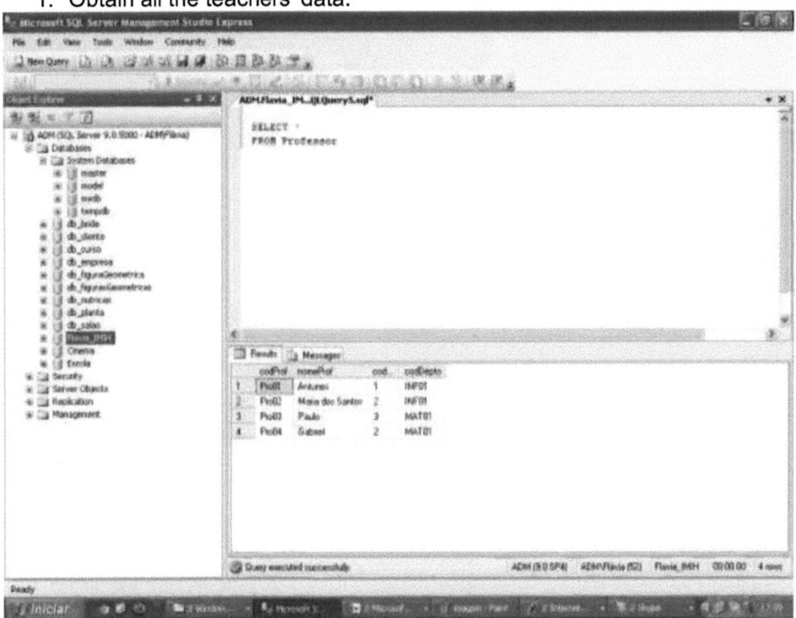

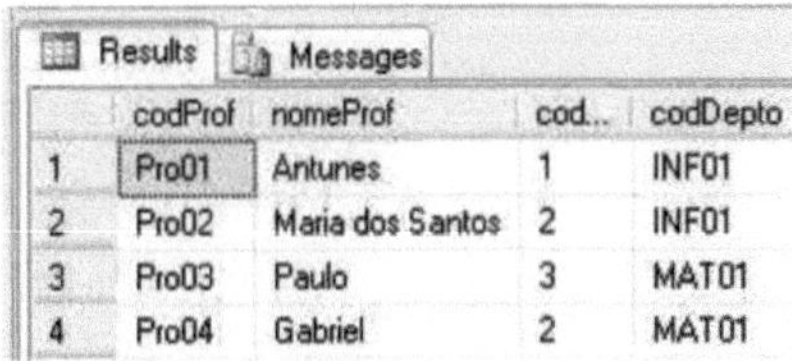

	codProf	nomeProf	cod...	codDepto
1	Pro01	Antunes	1	INF01
2	Pro02	Maria dos Santos	2	INF01
3	Pro03	Paulo	3	MAT01
4	Pro04	Gabriel	2	MAT01

2. Obtain the code and name of the teachers.

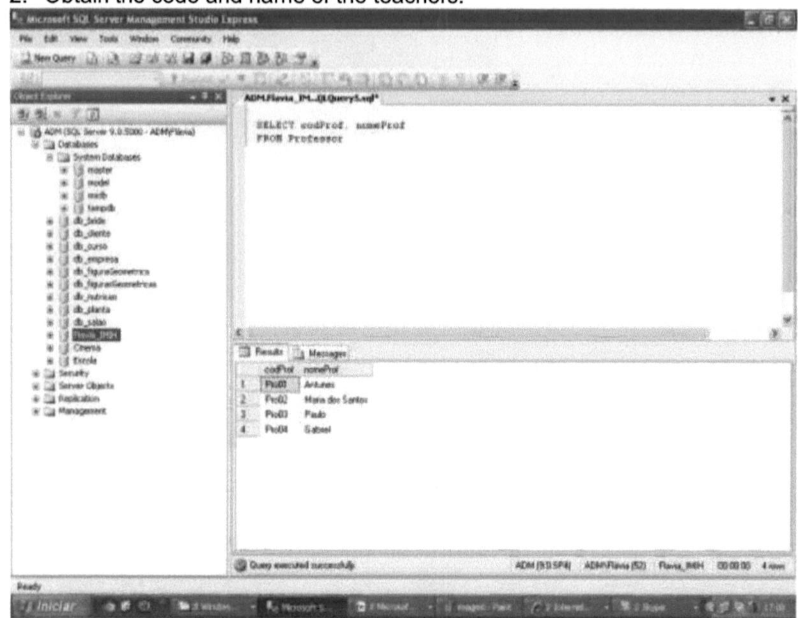

```
ADM.Flavia_IM...QLQuery5.sql*

SELECT codProf, nomeProf
FROM Professor
```

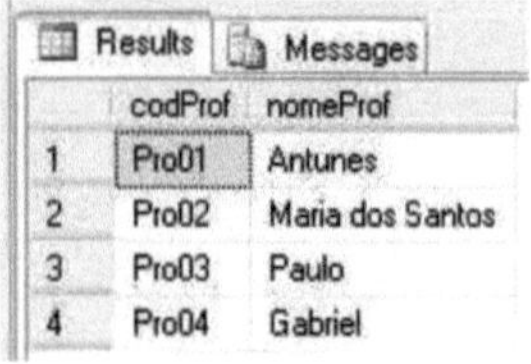

	codProf	nomeProf
1	Pro01	Antunes
2	Pro02	Maria dos Santos
3	Pro03	Paulo
4	Pro04	Gabriel

10

3. Obtain class capacity

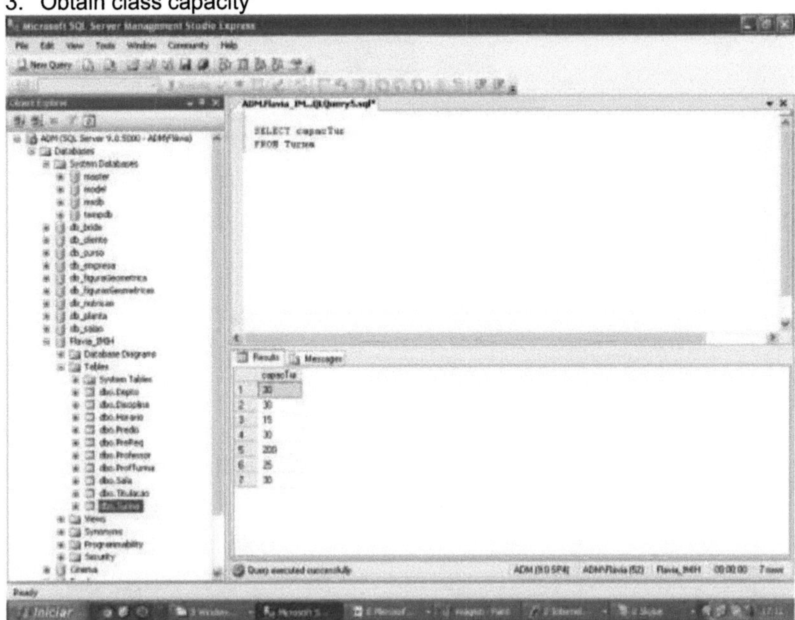

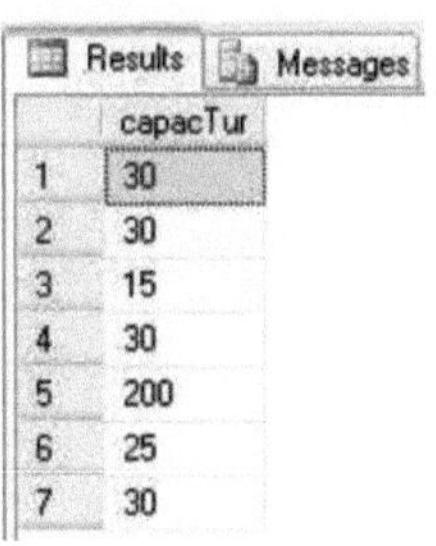

	capacTur
1	30
2	30
3	15
4	30
5	200
6	25
7	30

4. Obtain the different class capacity values.

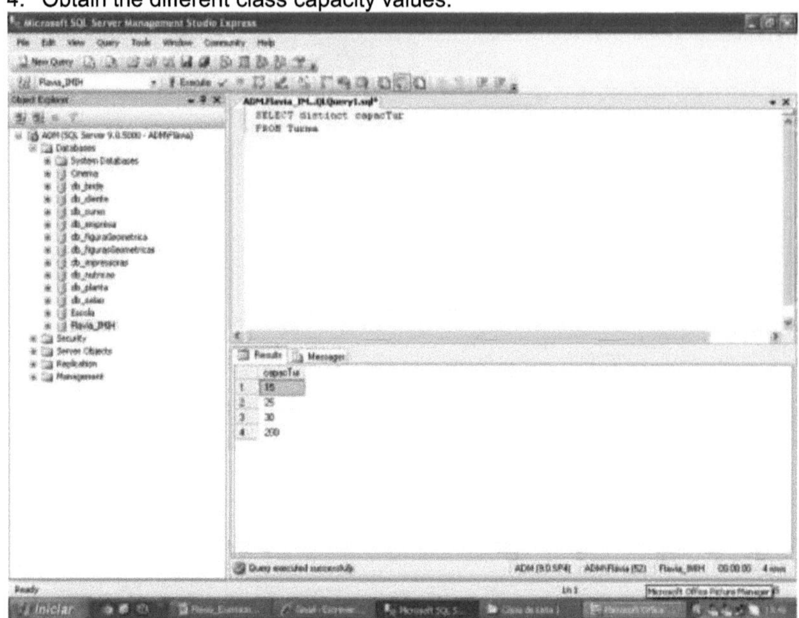

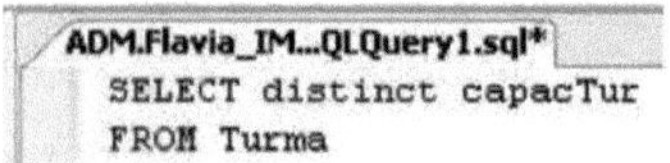

ADM.Flavia_IM...QLQuery1.sql*

```
SELECT distinct capacTur
FROM Turma
```

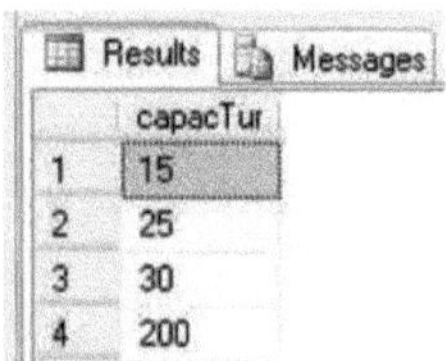

	capacTur
1	15
2	25
3	30
4	200

5. Obtain the name of the subjects in the INF01 department, provided they have more than 5 credits.

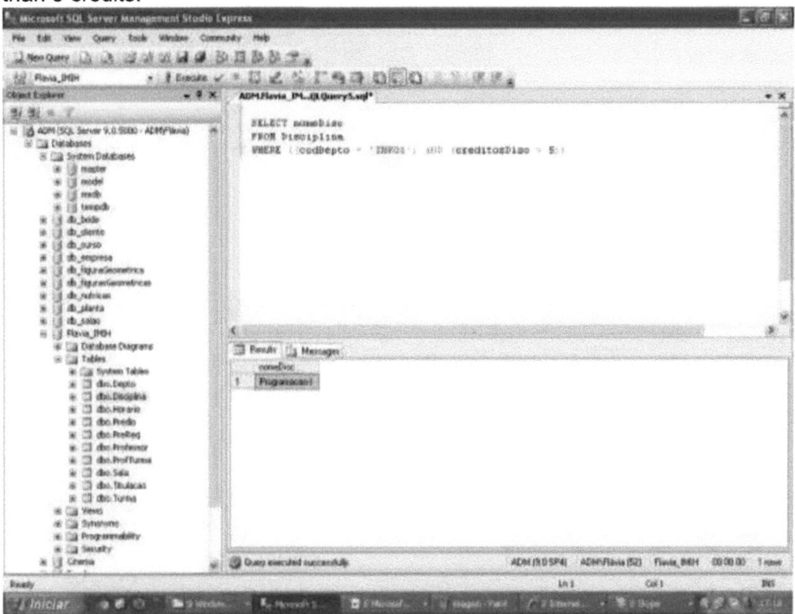

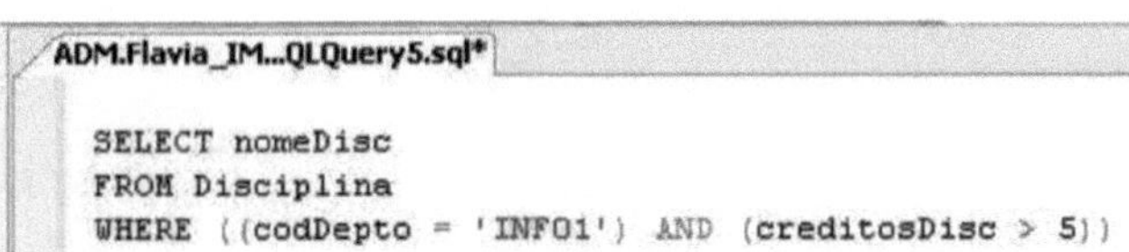

6. Get the code for the building called Laboratories.

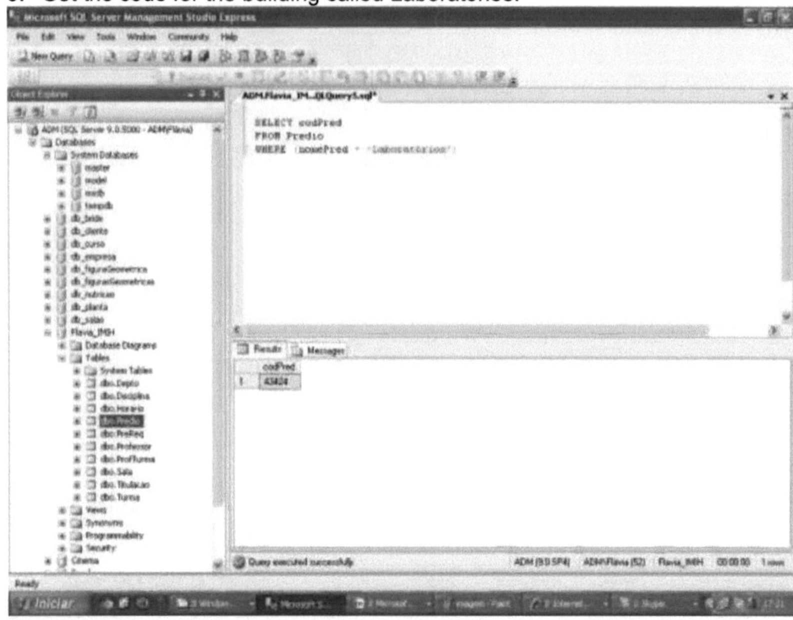

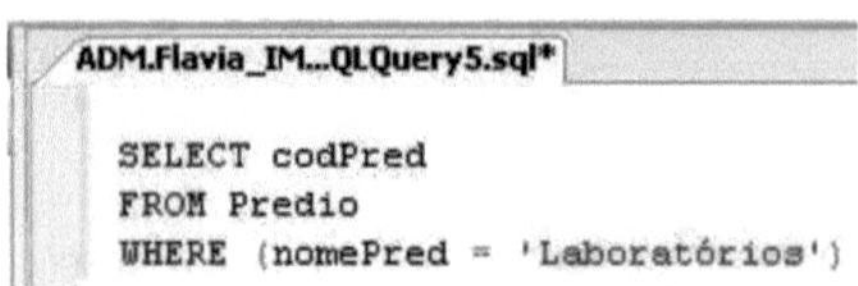

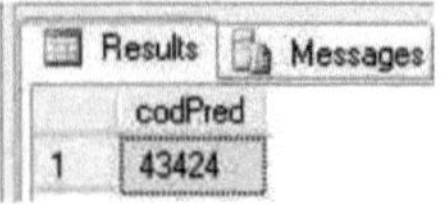

7. Obtain the room code and the building code, provided the room has a capacity of more than 35 seats.

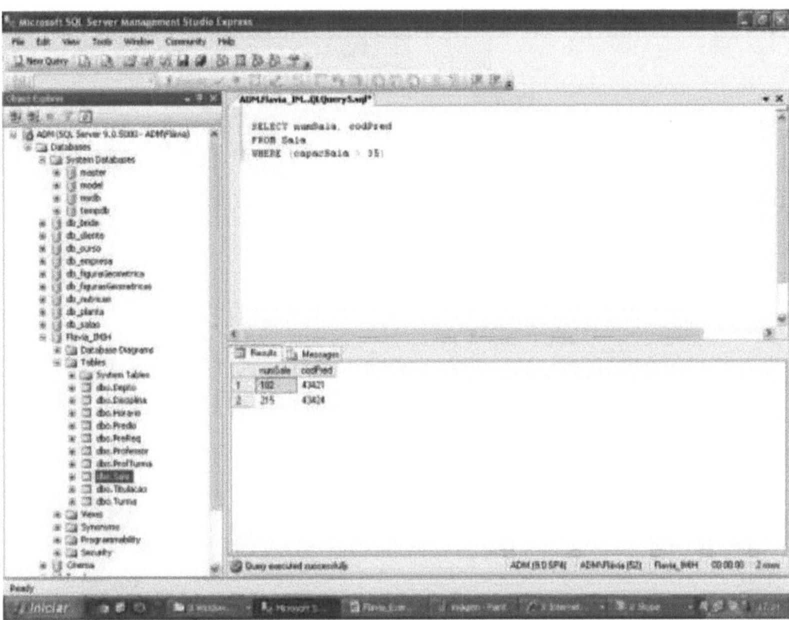

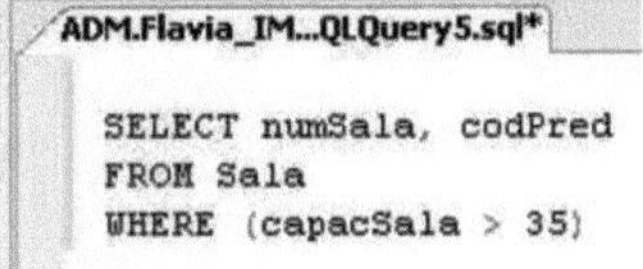

```
SELECT numSala, codPred
FROM Sala
WHERE (capacSala > 35)
```

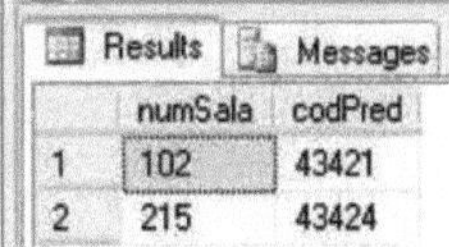

	numSala	codPred
1	102	43421
2	215	43424

8. Obtain the names of the professors who have degree 1 and who work in the INF01 department.

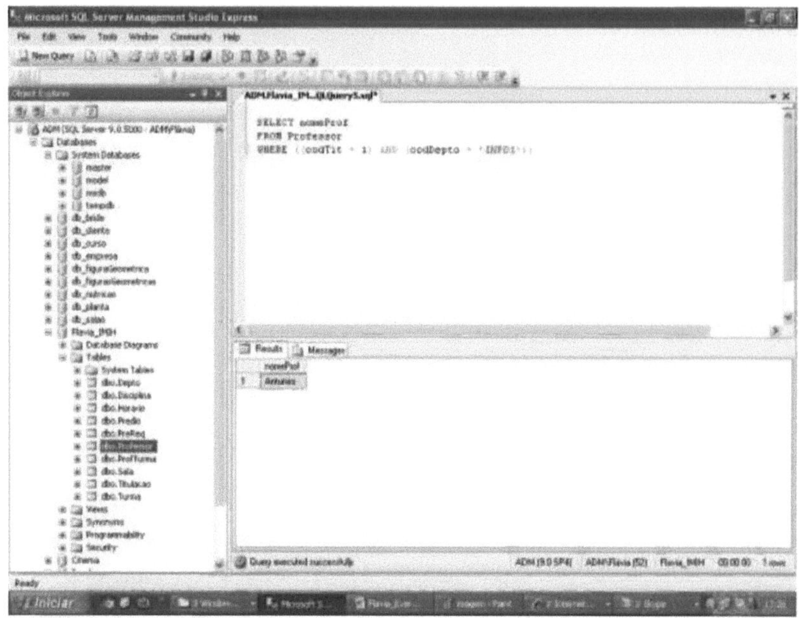

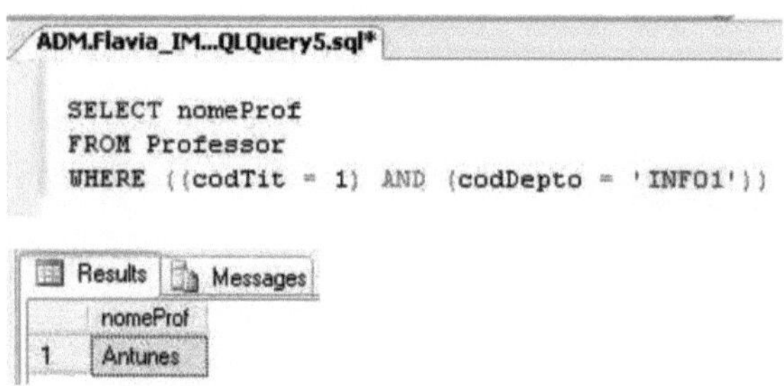

9. Obtain the names of the professors who have degree 2 or who work in the INF01 department.

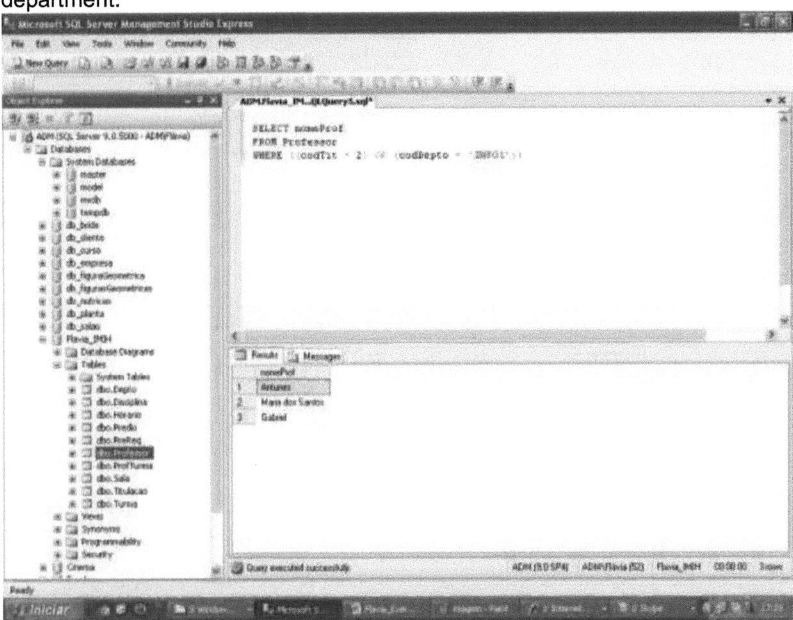

ADM.Flavia_IM...QLQuery5.sql*

```sql
SELECT nomeProf
FROM Professor
WHERE ((codTit = 2) OR (codDepto = 'INF01'))
```

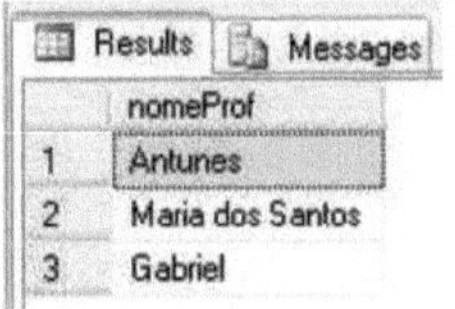

	Results	Messages
	nomeProf	
1	Antunes	
2	Maria dos Santos	
3	Gabriel	

10. Return the code and the name of the teachers who have the surname Santos.

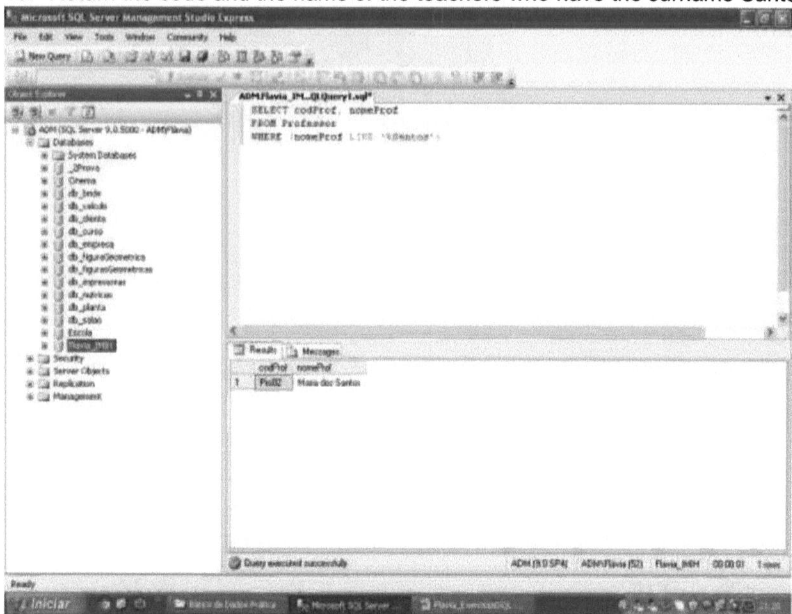

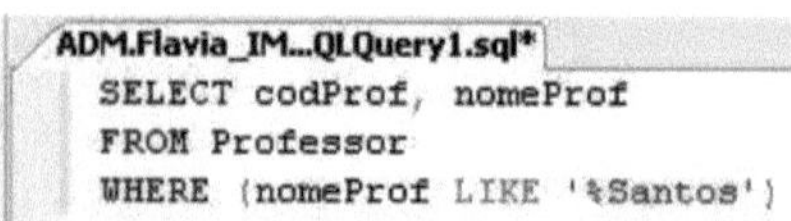

```
ADM.Flavia_IM...QLQuery1.sql*
    SELECT codProf, nomeProf
    FROM Professor
    WHERE (nomeProf LIKE '%Santos')
```

	codProf	nomeProf
1	Pro02	Maria dos Santos

11. Knowing that each course credit corresponds to 15 hours of tuition, return the name of the course and its number of hours of tuition.

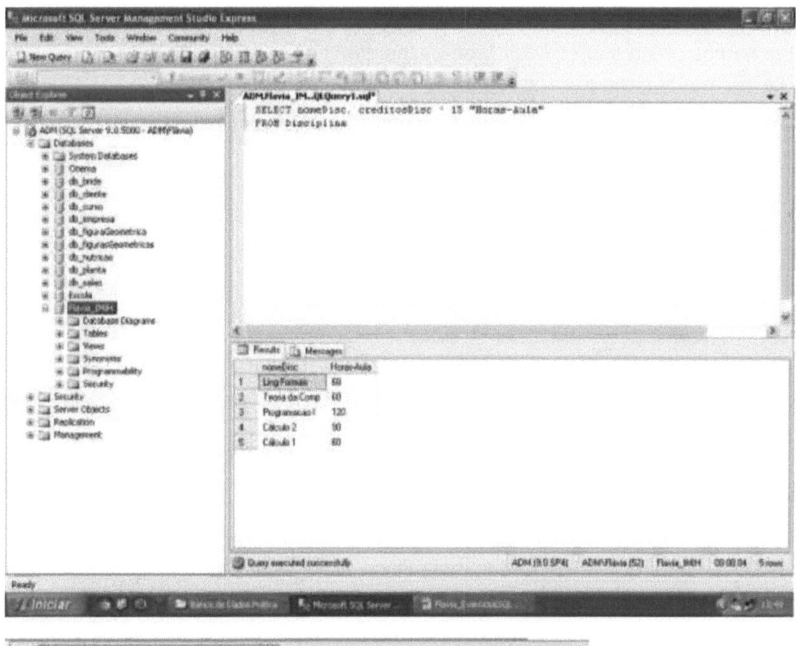

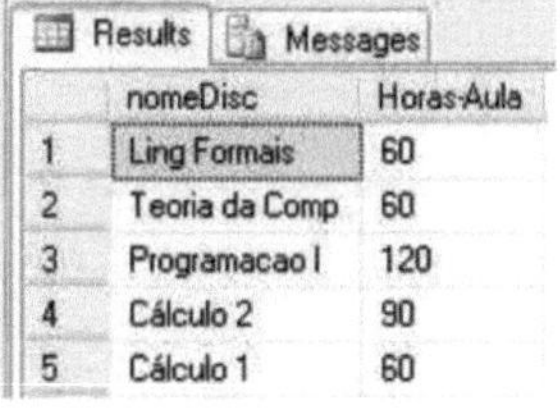

ADM.Flavia_IM...QLQuery1.sql*

```sql
SELECT nomeDisc, creditosDisc * 15 "Horas-Aula"
FROM Disciplina
```

	nomeDisc	Horas-Aula
1	Ling Formais	60
2	Teoria da Comp	60
3	Programacao I	120
4	Cálculo 2	90
5	Cálculo 1	60

CHAPTER 3

List 02

1.   Get the names of the subjects followed by the name of your department.

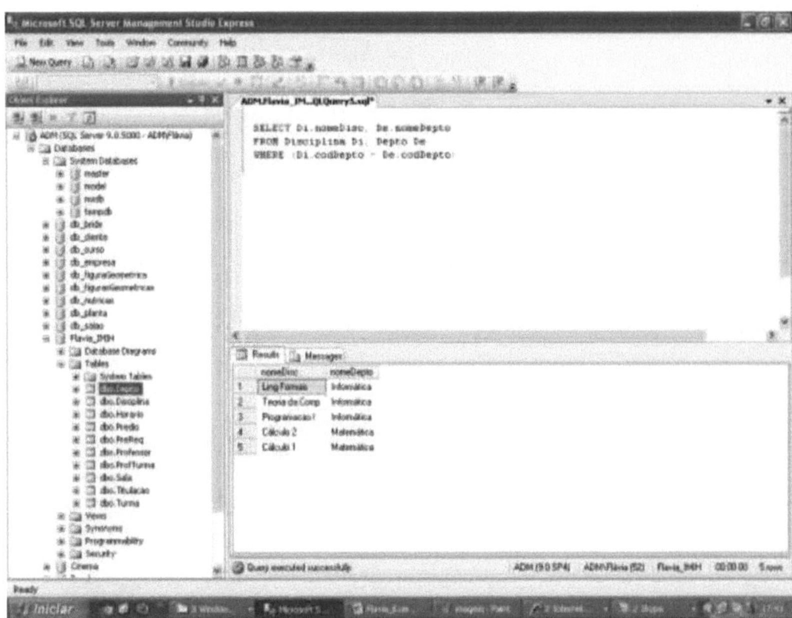

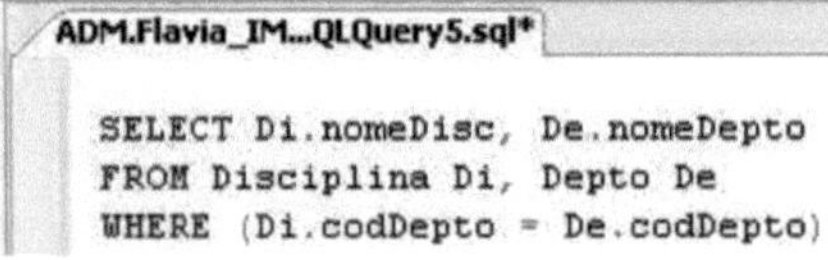

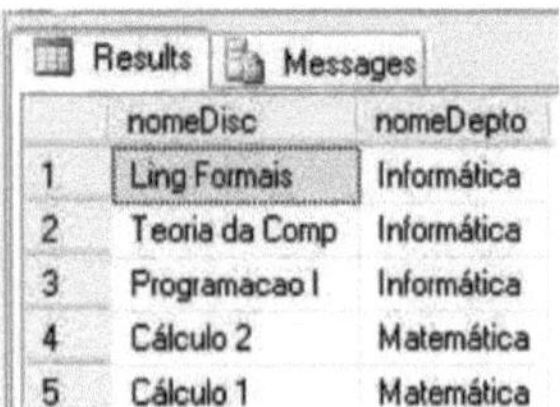

2.   Get the names of the professors who hold the title 'Dr'.

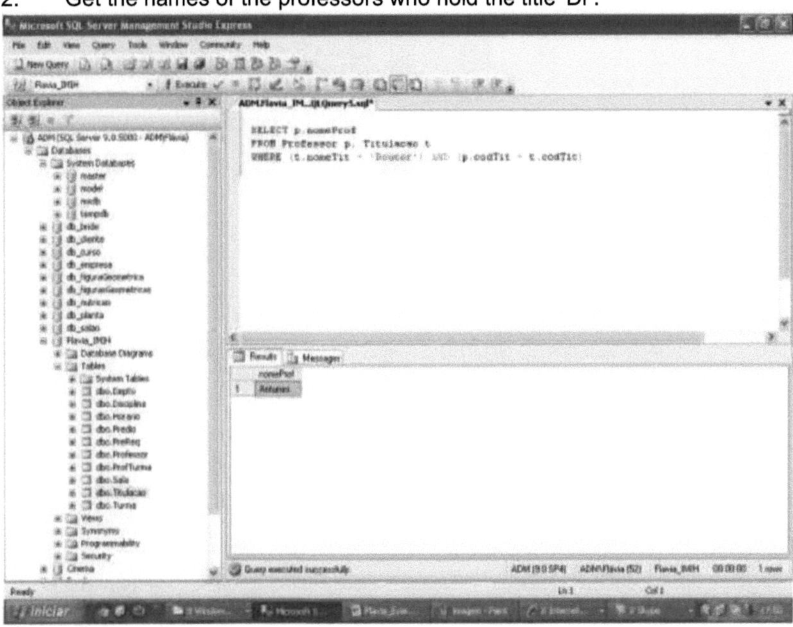

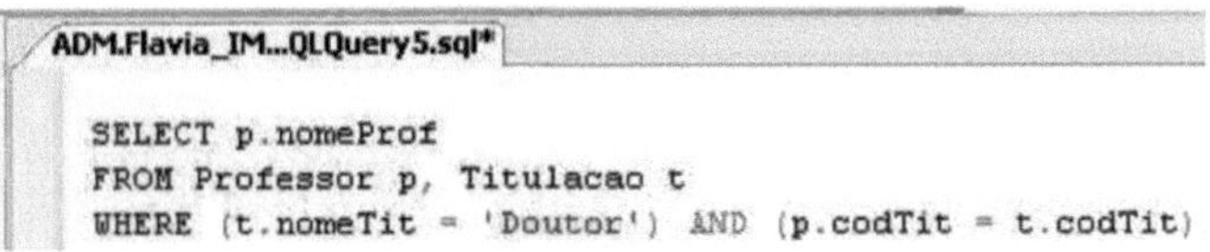

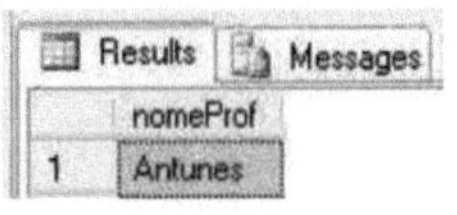

3. Get the names of the teachers who taught in 1999/2.

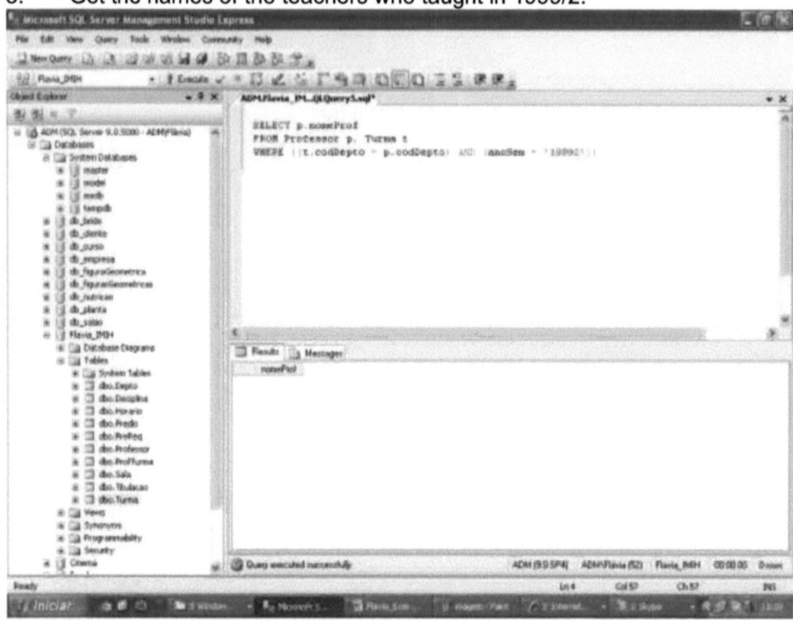

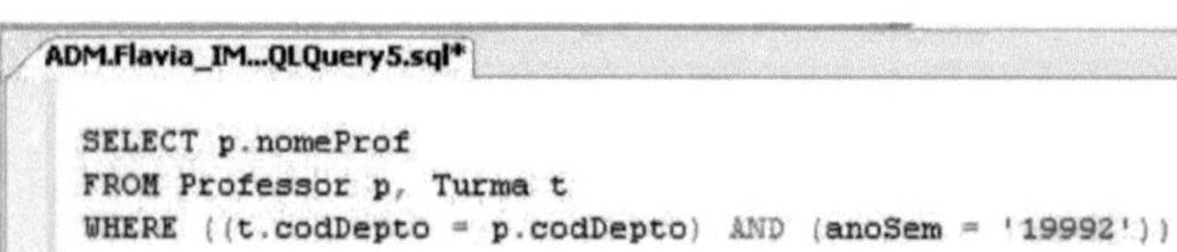

ADM.Flavia_IM...QLQuery5.sql*

```
SELECT p.nomeProf
FROM Professor p, Turma t
WHERE ((t.codDepto = p.codDepto) AND (anoSem = '19992'))
```

4.   Get the numbers of the rooms in the building named 'Laboratories' whose capacity is greater than 30.

```
ADM.Flavia_IM...QLQuery1.sql*
  SELECT s.numSala
  FROM Sala s, Predio p
  WHERE ((s.codPred = p.codPred) AND (p.nomePred = 'Laboratórios') AND (s.capacSala > 30))
```

	numSala
1	215

5.   Get the names of the courses that were offered in 2000/1.

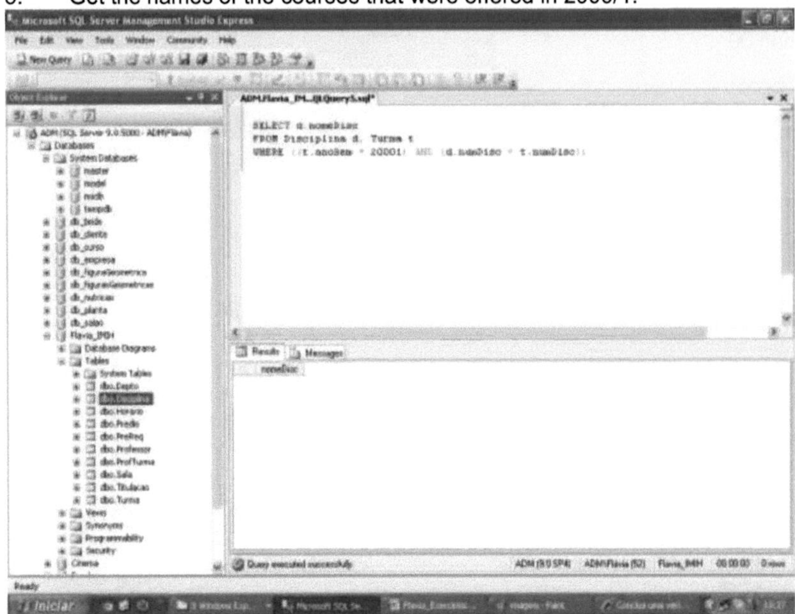

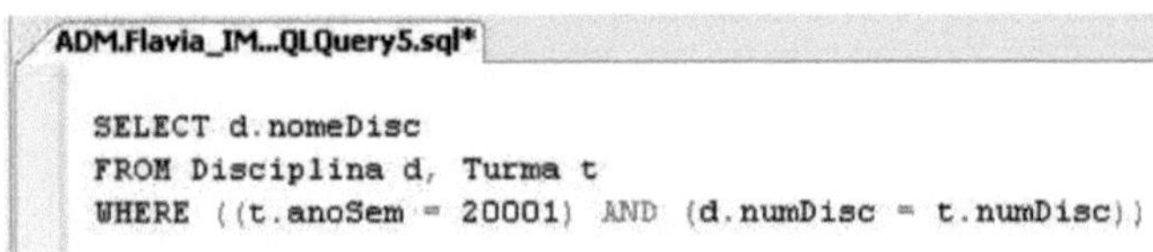

6. Get the numbers of the rooms in the "Laboratories" building.

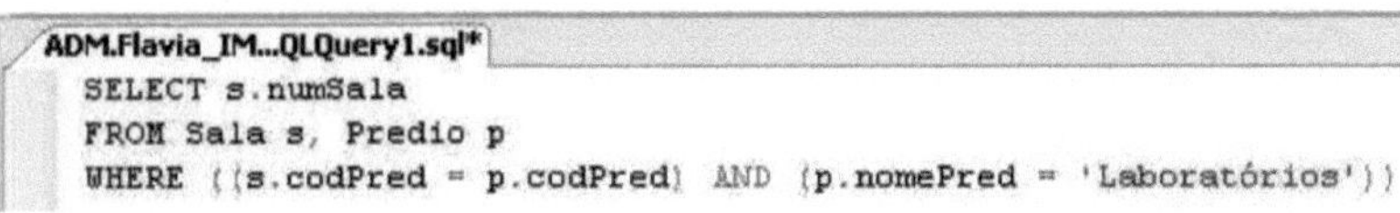

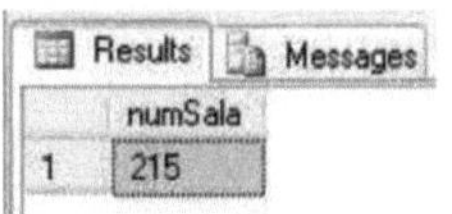

7.   Get the names of the professors followed by the name of their department.

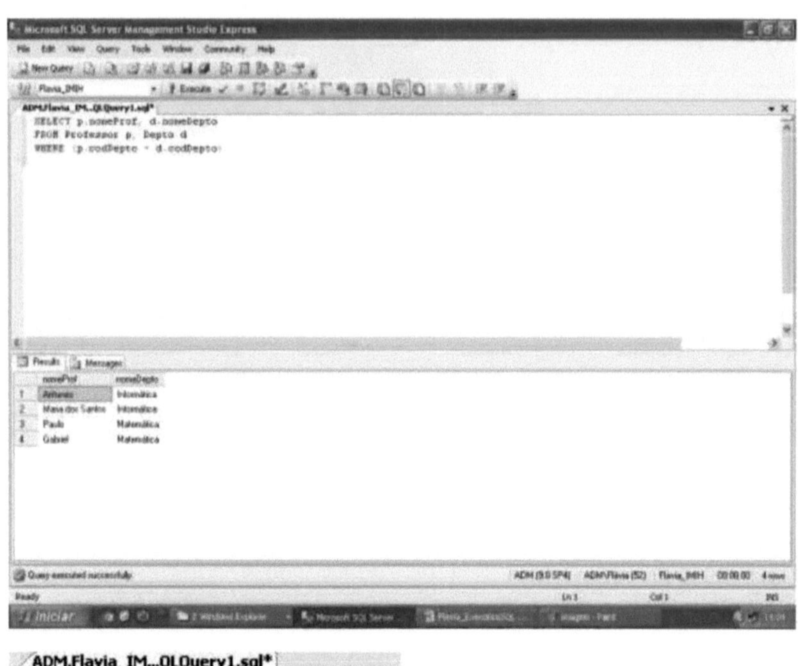

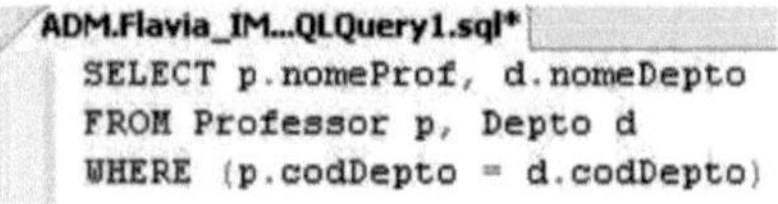

ADM.Flavia_IM...QLQuery1.sql*

```sql
SELECT p.nomeProf, d.nomeDepto
FROM Professor p, Depto d
WHERE (p.codDepto = d.codDepto)
```

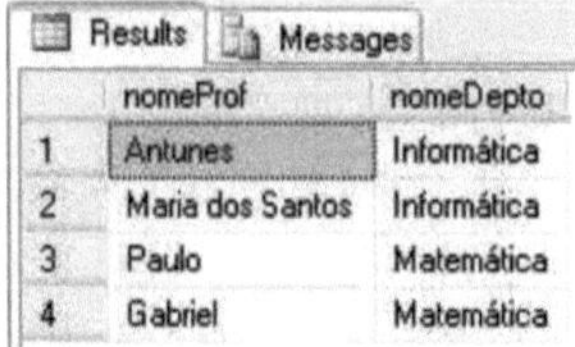

	nomeProf	nomeDepto
1	Antunes	Informática
2	Maria dos Santos	Informática
3	Paulo	Matemática
4	Gabriel	Matemática

8. Get the codes of the teachers who don't have a class in 1999/2.

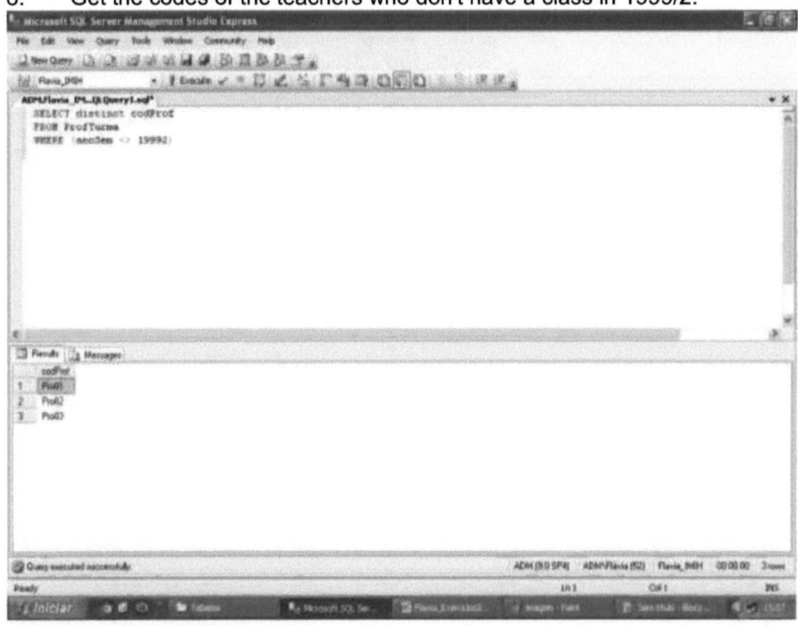

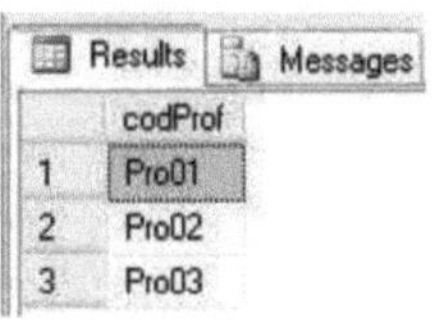

ADM.Flavia_IM...QLQuery1.sql*

```sql
SELECT distinct codProf
FROM ProfTurma
WHERE (anoSem <> 19992)
```

	Results	Messages
	codProf	
1	Pro01	
2	Pro02	
3	Pro03	

9. Names of departments with subjects that do not have a prerequisite.

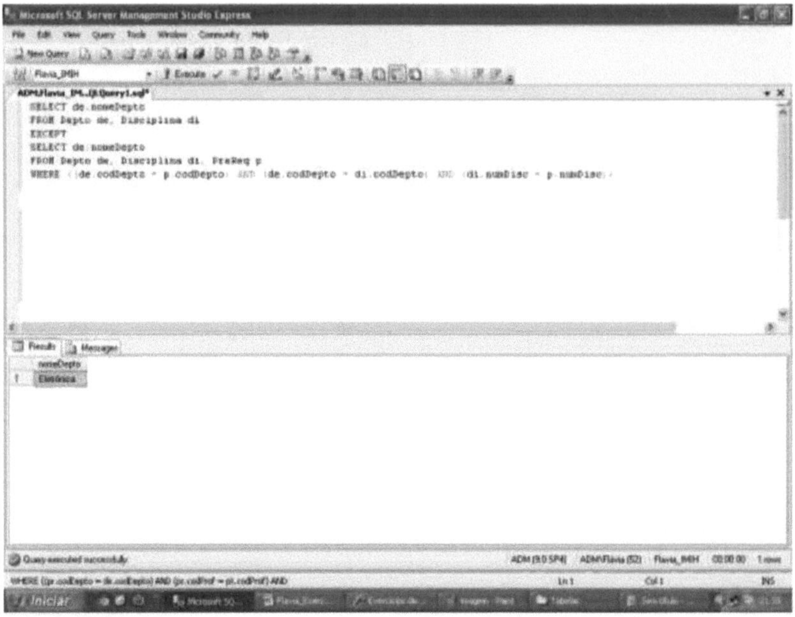

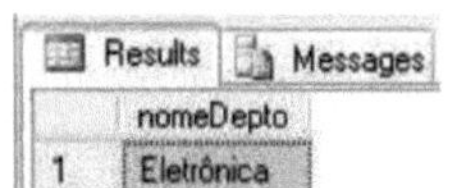

```
ADM.Flavia_IM...QLQuery1.sql*
    SELECT de.nomeDepto
    FROM Depto de, Disciplina di
    EXCEPT
    SELECT de.nomeDepto
    FROM Depto de, Disciplina di, PreReq p
    WHERE ((de.codDepto = p.codDepto) AND (de.codDepto = di.codDepto) AND (di.numDisc = p.numDisc))
```

Results	Messages
nomeDepto	
1	Eletrônica

10. Get the codes of the teachers who taught in 1999/2 and 2000/1.

ADM.Flavia_IM...QLQuery1.sql*

```sql
SELECT codProf
FROM ProfTurma
WHERE ((anoSem = 19992) AND (anoSem = 20001))
```

Results | Messages

codProf

11. Get the names of the departments in which there is at least one subject with more than three credits.

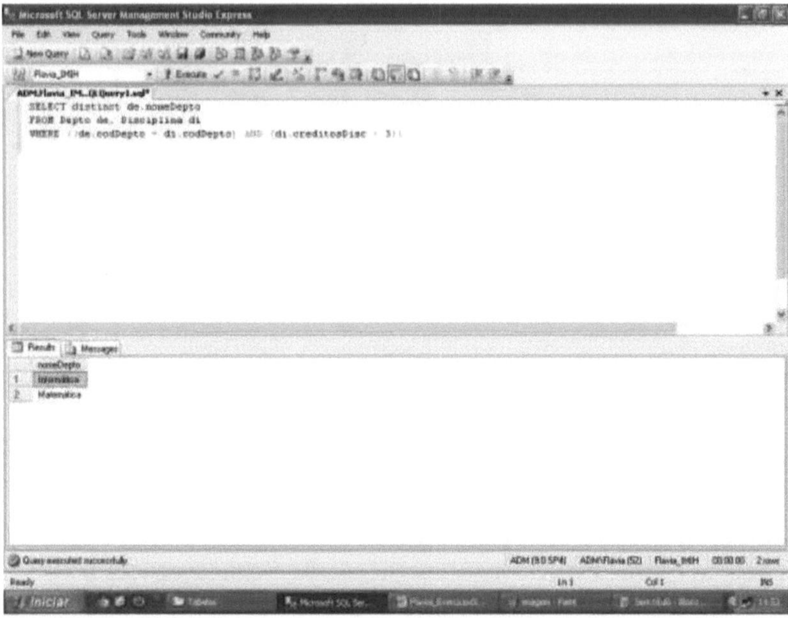

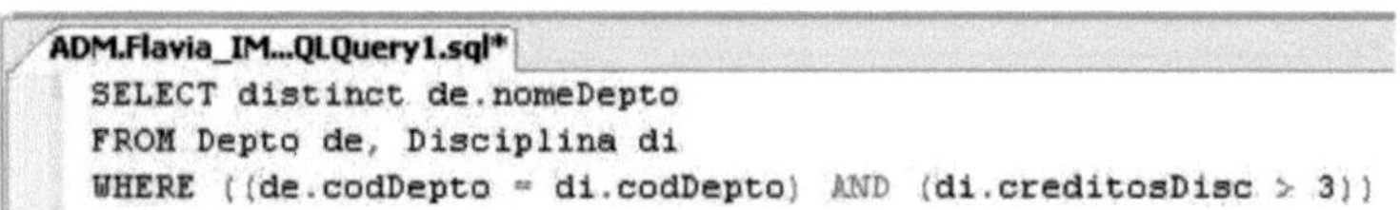

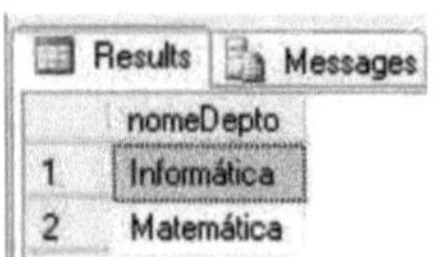

CHAPTER 4

List 03

1. Obtain the codes of the different departments that have classes in the year-semester 2002/1

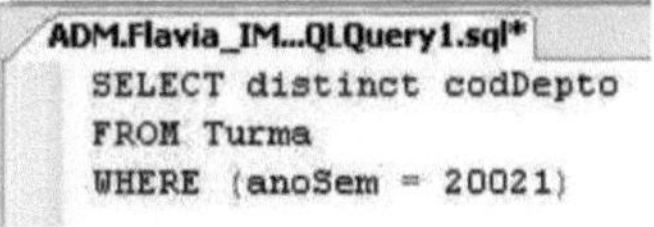

```
ADM.Flavia_IM...QLQuery1.sql*
    SELECT distinct codDepto
    FROM Turma
    WHERE (anoSem = 20021)
```

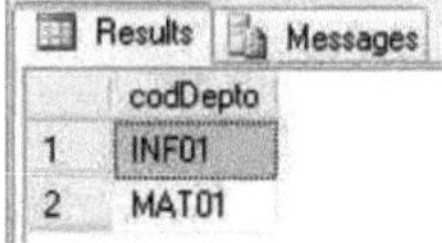

	codDepto
1	INF01
2	MAT01

2. Obtain the codes of the professors who are from the department code 'INFOT and who taught at least one class in 2002/1.

ADM.Flavia_IM...QLQuery1.sql*

```sql
SELECT distinct p.codProf
FROM Professor p, ProfTurma pt
WHERE ((p.codProf = pt.codProf) AND (pt.anoSem = 20021) AND (p.codDepto = 'INFO1'))
```

	codProf
1	Pro01
2	Pro02

3. Obtain the class timetables (day of the week, starting time and number of hours taught) of Professor "Antunes" in 2002/1.

```
ADM.Flavia_IM...QLQuery1.sql*
    SELECT distinct h.DiaSem, h.HoraInicio, h.NumHoras
    FROM  Professor p, ProfTurma pt, Horario h
    WHERE ((p.NomeProf = 'Antunes') AND (h.anoSem = 20021) AND
    (p.codProf = pt.codProf) AND (pt.anoSem = h.anoSem) AND (pt.codDepto = h.codDepto)
    AND (pt.numDisc = h.numDisc) AND (pt.siglaTur = h.siglaTur))
```

	DiaSem	HoraInicio	NumHoras
1	2	10:30	60
2	4	13:30	60

4. Obtain the names of the departments that have classes that, in 2002/1, have classes in room 101 of the building called 'Informatics-Classes'.

ADM.Flavia_IM...QLQuery1.sql*

```sql
SELECT distinct d.nomeDepto
FROM Depto d, Horario h, Predio p
WHERE ((h.codDepto = d.codDepto) AND (h.anoSem = 20021) AND (h.numSala = 101)
AND (p.codPred = h.codPredio) AND (p.nomePred = 'Informática-Aulas'))
```

	nomeDepto
1	Informática

5. Obtain the codes of the professors with the title 'Doctor' who did not teach in 2002/1.

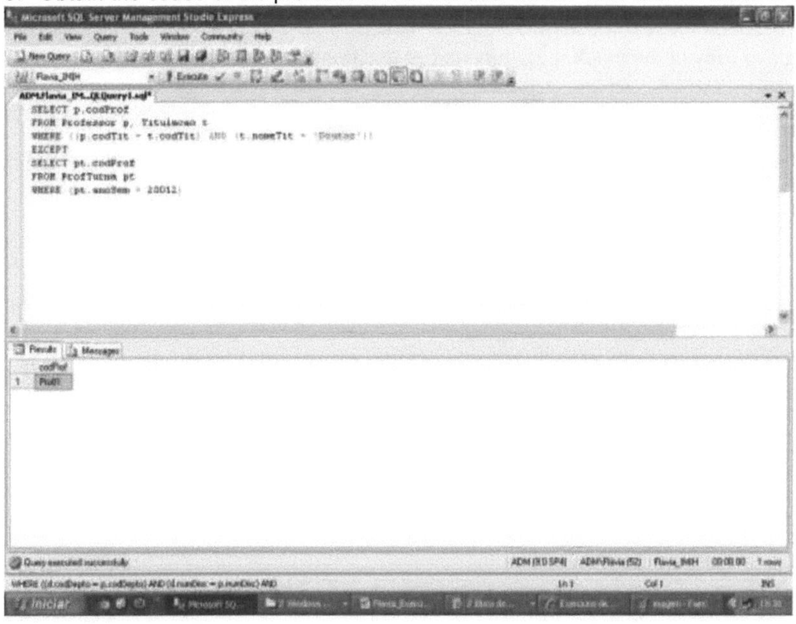

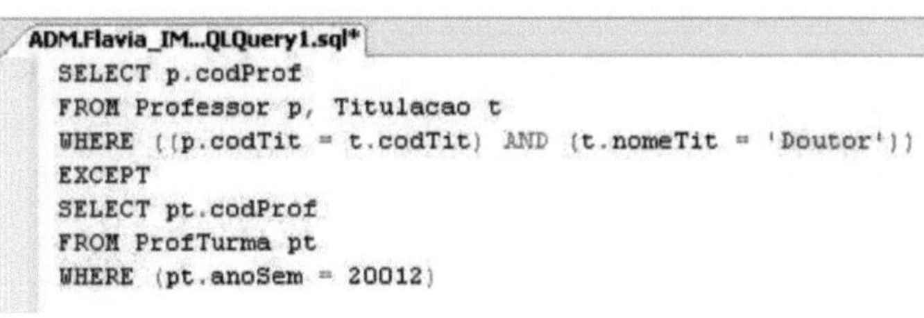

```
ADM.Flavia_IM...QLQuery1.sql*
    SELECT p.codProf
    FROM Professor p, Titulacao t
    WHERE ((p.codTit = t.codTit) AND (t.nomeTit = 'Doutor'))
    EXCEPT
    SELECT pt.codProf
    FROM ProfTurma pt
    WHERE (pt.anoSem = 20012)
```

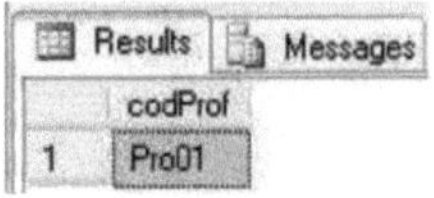

	codProf
1	Pro01

6. Obtain the room identifiers (building code and room number) that in 2002/1:

a) on Mondays (day of the week = 2), they had at least one class in the 'Computer Science' department,

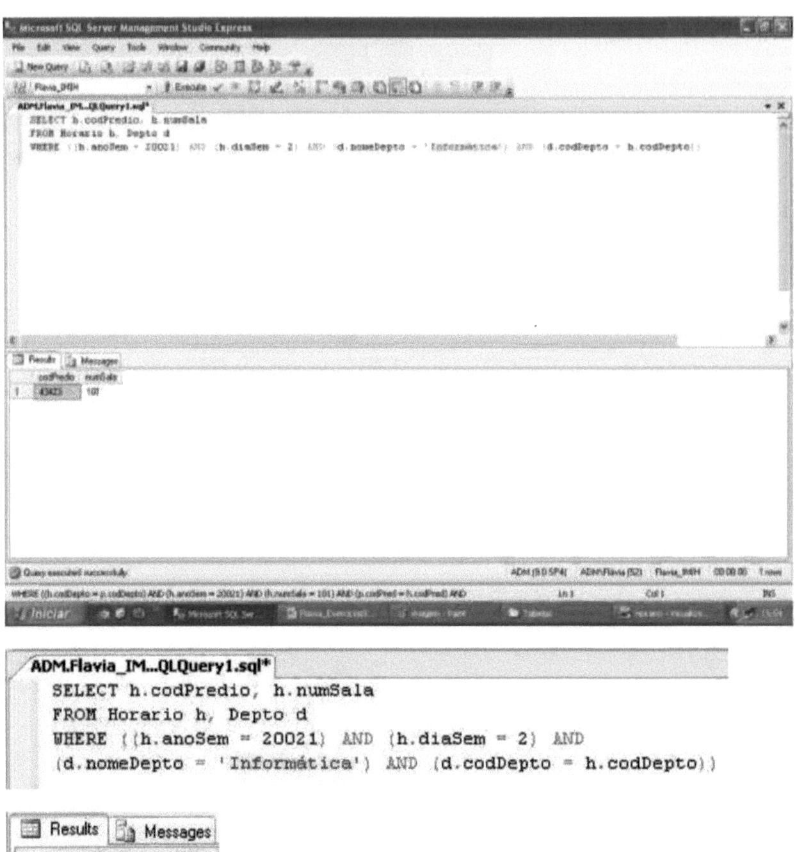

```
ADM.Flavia_IM...QLQuery1.sql*
    SELECT h.codPredio, h.numSala
    FROM Horario h, Depto d
    WHERE ((h.anoSem = 20021) AND (h.diaSem = 2) AND
    (d.nomeDepto = 'Informática') AND (d.codDepto = h.codDepto))
```

	Results	Messages	
		codPredio	numSala
1		43423	101

b) on Wednesdays (day of the week = 4), had at least one class taught by the teacher called 'Antunes'.

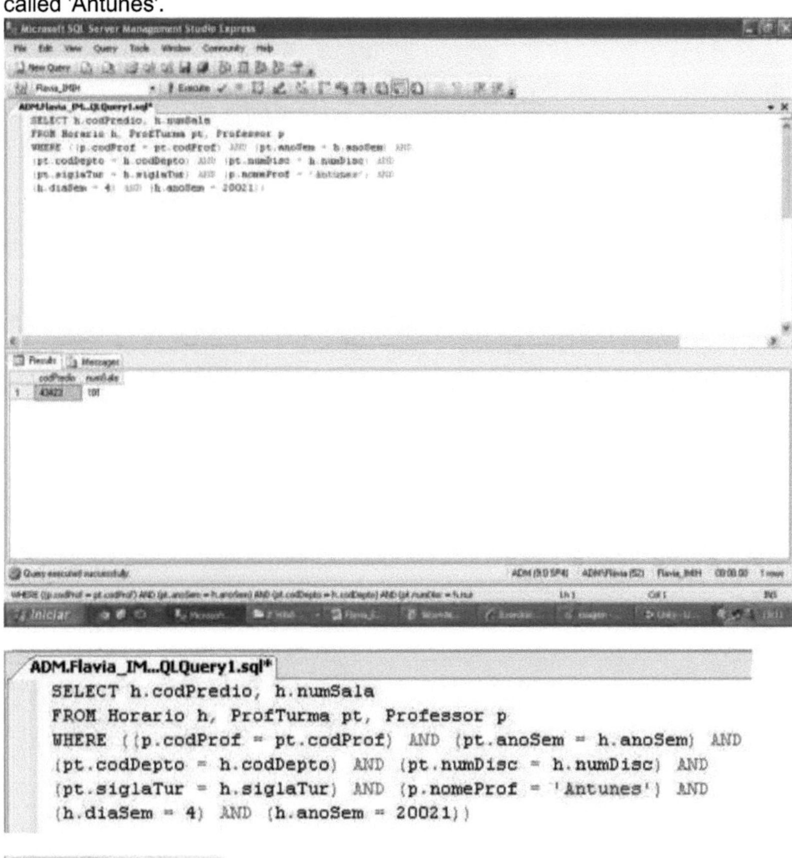

```
ADM.Flavia_IM...QLQuery1.sql*
    SELECT h.codPredio, h.numSala
    FROM Horario h, ProfTurma pt, Professor p
    WHERE ((p.codProf = pt.codProf) AND (pt.anoSem = h.anoSem) AND
    (pt.codDepto = h.codDepto) AND (pt.numDisc = h.numDisc) AND
    (pt.siglaTur = h.siglaTur) AND (p.nomeProf = 'Antunes') AND
    (h.diaSem = 4) AND (h.anoSem = 20021))
```

	codPredio	numSala
1	43423	101

7. Get the day of the week, the start time and the number of hours in each timetable for each class taught by a teacher called 'Antunes' in 2002/1, in room number 101 of building code 43423.

```
ADM.Flavia_IM...QLQuery1.sql*
SELECT h.diaSem, h.horaInicio, h.numHoras
FROM Professor p, ProfTurma pt, Horario h
WHERE ((p.codProf = pt.codProf) AND (pt.anoSem = h.anoSem) AND
(pt.codDepto = h.codDepto) AND (pt.numDisc = h.numDisc) AND
(pt.siglaTur = h.siglaTur) AND (h.numSala = 101) AND
(pt.anoSem = 20021) AND (p.nomeProf = 'Antunes') AND (h.codPredio = 43423))
```

	diaSem	horaInicio	numHoras
1	2	10:30	60
2	4	13:30	60

8. For each subject that has a prerequisite, get the name of the subject followed by the name of the subject that is its prerequisite.

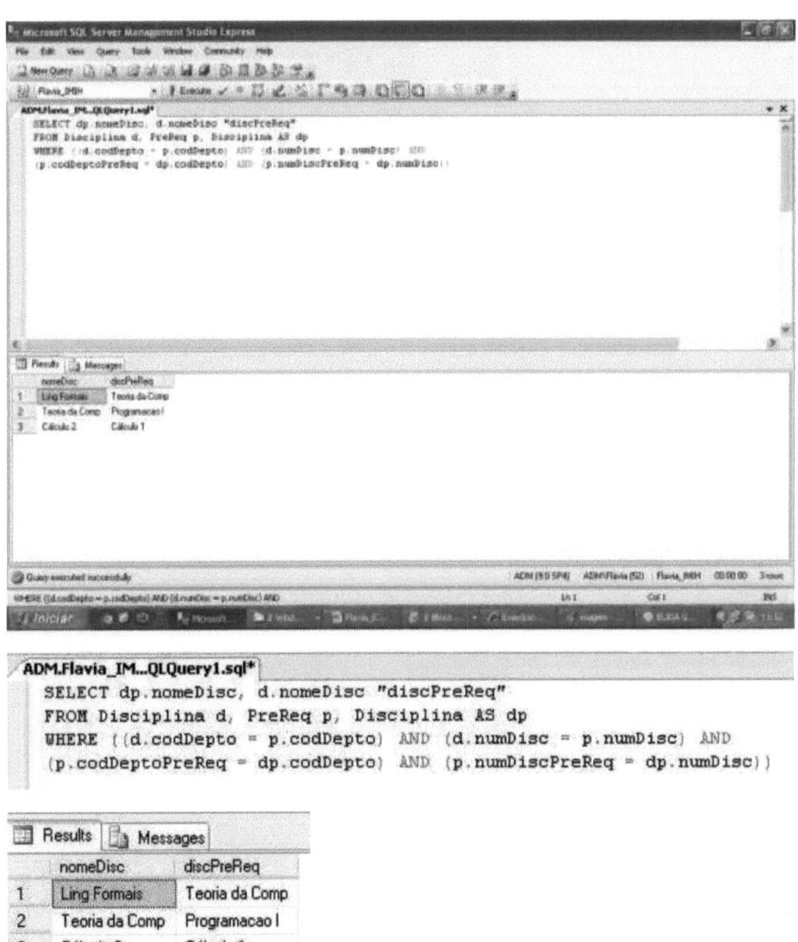

ADM.Flavia_IM...QLQuery1.sql*

```sql
SELECT dp.nomeDisc, d.nomeDisc "discPreReq"
FROM Disciplina d, PreReq p, Disciplina AS dp
WHERE ((d.codDepto = p.codDepto) AND (d.numDisc = p.numDisc) AND
(p.codDeptoPreReq = dp.codDepto) AND (p.numDiscPreReq = dp.numDisc))
```

	nomeDisc	discPreReq
1	Ling Formais	Teoria da Comp
2	Teoria da Comp	Programacao I
3	Cálculo 2	Cálculo 1

9. Obtain the names of the subjects that are not prerequisites.

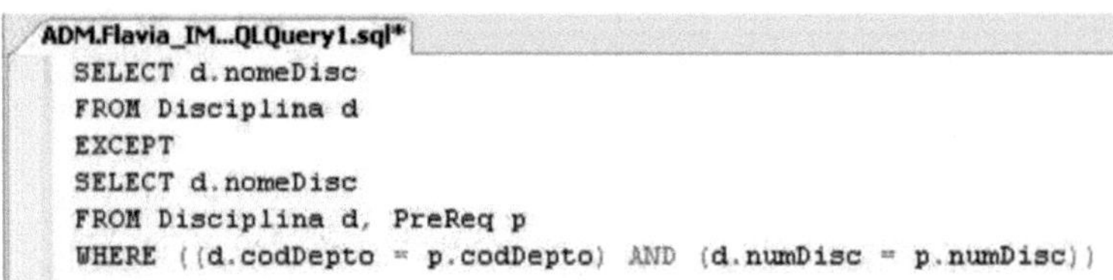

```
ADM.Flavia_IM...QLQuery1.sql*
SELECT d.nomeDisc
FROM Disciplina d
EXCEPT
SELECT d.nomeDisc
FROM Disciplina d, PreReq p
WHERE ((d.codDepto = p.codDepto) AND (d.numDisc = p.numDisc))
```

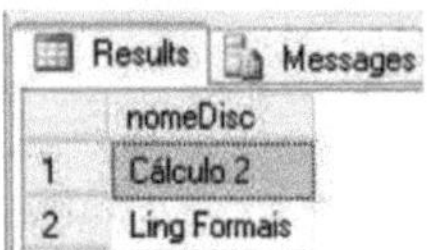

	nomeDisc
1	Cálculo 2
2	Ling Formais

10. Obtain the names of teachers whose titles have a code other than 3.

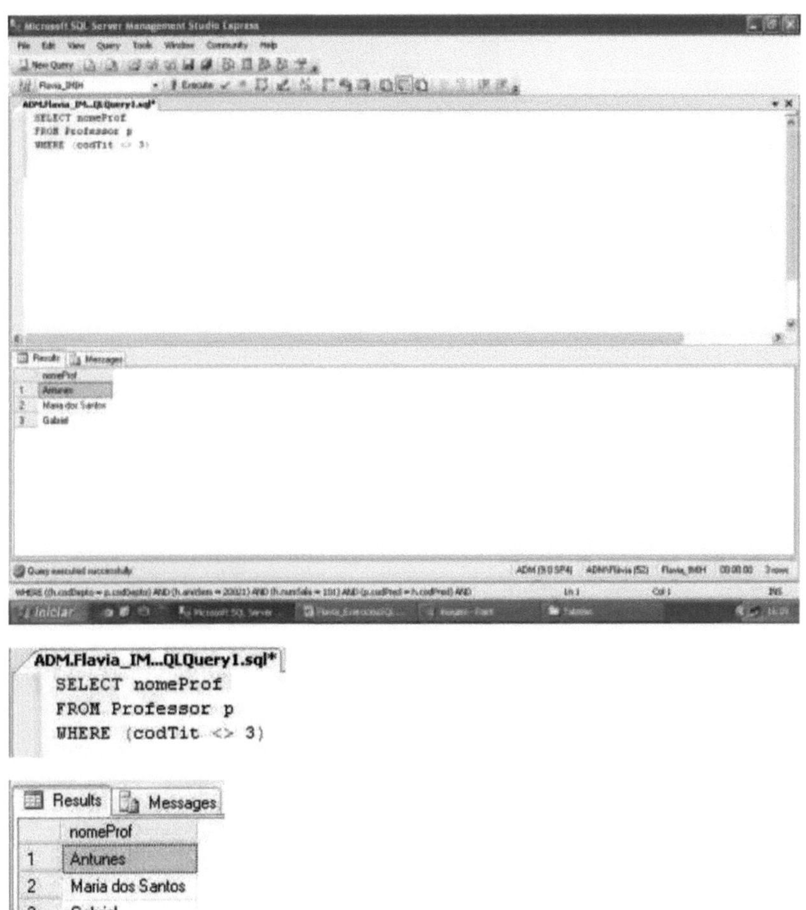

ADM.Flavia_IM...QLQuery1.sql*
```sql
SELECT nomeProf
FROM Professor p
WHERE (codTit <> 3)
```

	nomeProf
1	Antunes
2	Maria dos Santos
3	Gabriel

11. Obtain the names of the departments that have classes that, in 2002/1, have classes in room 101 of the building called 'Informatics-Classes'.

```
ADM.Flavia_IM...QLQuery1.sql*
    SELECT distinct d.nomeDepto
    FROM Depto d, Horario h, Predio p
    WHERE ((d.codDepto = h.codDepto) AND (h.anoSem = 20021) AND (h.numSala = 101)
     AND (h.codPredio = p.codPred) AND (p.nomePred = 'Informática-Aulas'))
```

	Results	Messages
	nomeDepto	
1	Informática	

12. Get the name of each department followed by the name of each of its subjects that has more than three credits (if the department has no subjects or if the department has no subjects with more than three credits, its name should appear followed by empty).

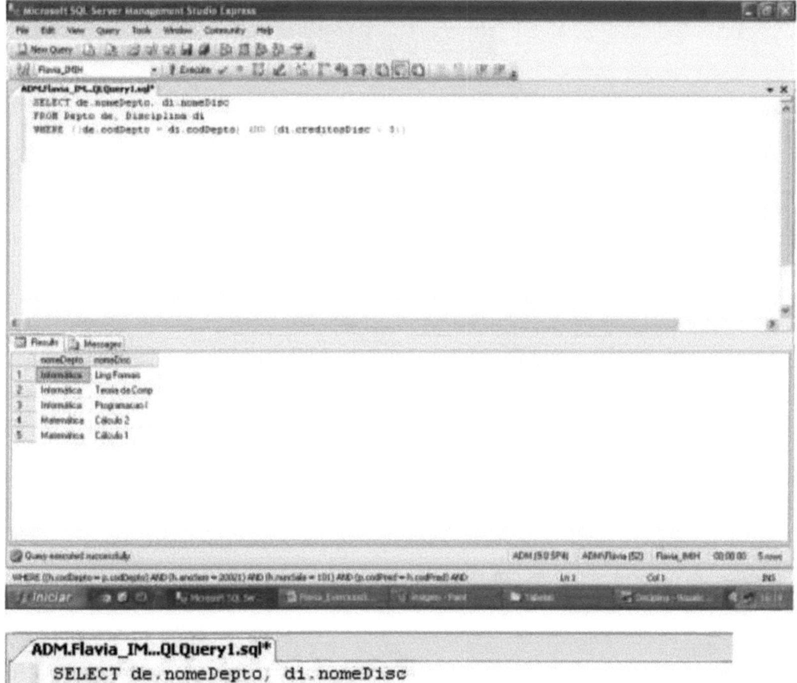

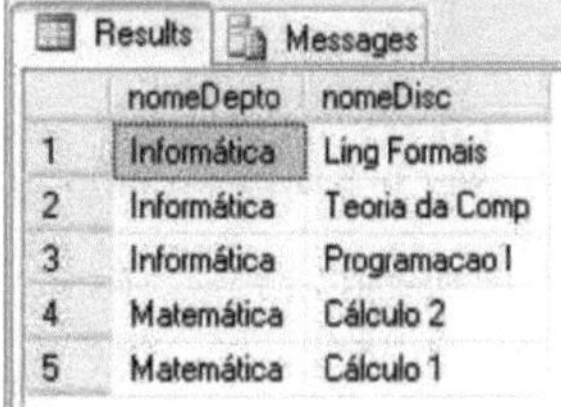

```
ADM.Flavia_IM...QLQuery1.sql*
    SELECT de.nomeDepto, di.nomeDisc
    FROM Depto de, Disciplina di
    WHERE ((de.codDepto = di.codDepto) AND (di.creditosDisc > 3))
```

	nomeDepto	nomeDisc
1	Informática	Ling Formais
2	Informática	Teoria da Comp
3	Informática	Programacao I
4	Matemática	Cálculo 2
5	Matemática	Cálculo 1

13. Obtain the names of the professors who are from the department called 'Informatics', who hold a doctorate, and who, in 2002/2, taught a course in the 'Informatics' department with more than three credits.

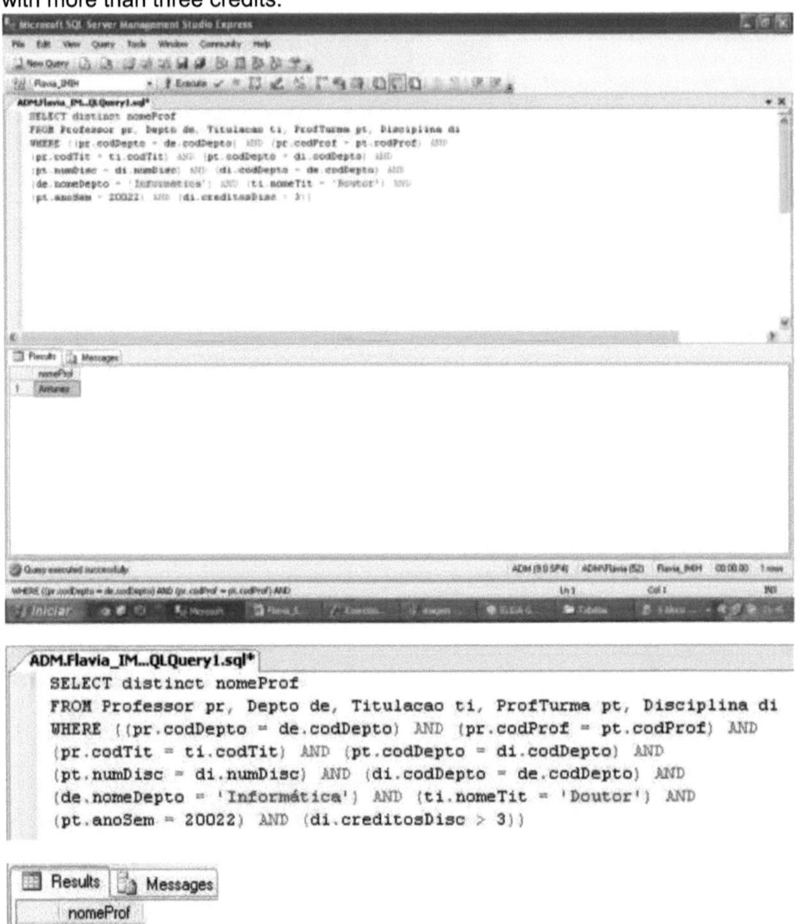

```
ADM.Flavia_IM...QLQuery1.sql*
    SELECT distinct nomeProf
    FROM Professor pr, Depto de, Titulacao ti, ProfTurma pt, Disciplina di
    WHERE ((pr.codDepto = de.codDepto) AND (pr.codProf = pt.codProf) AND
    (pr.codTit = ti.codTit) AND (pt.codDepto = di.codDepto) AND
    (pt.numDisc = di.numDisc) AND (di.codDepto = de.codDepto) AND
    (de.nomeDepto = 'Informática') AND (ti.nomeTit = 'Doutor') AND
    (pt.anoSem = 20022) AND (di.creditosDisc > 3))
```

Results	Messages
nomeProf	
1	Antunes

14. Get the number of subjects in the department called 'Informatics[*1].

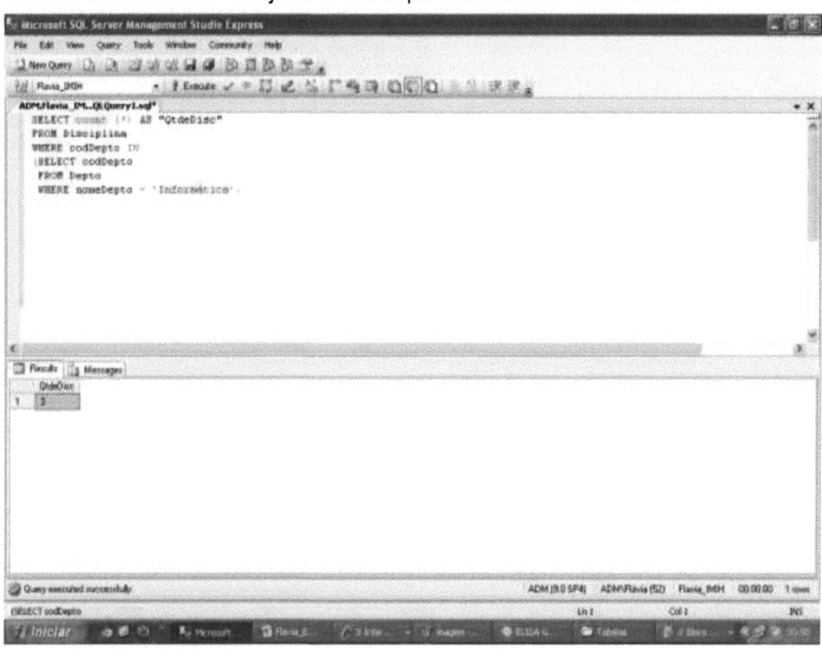

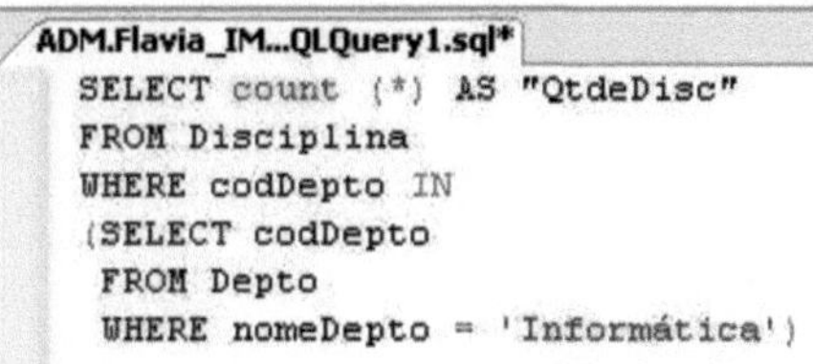

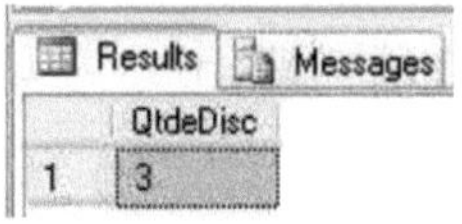

15. Obtain the names of the subjects in the department called 'Informatics' that have the highest number of credits among the subjects in this department.

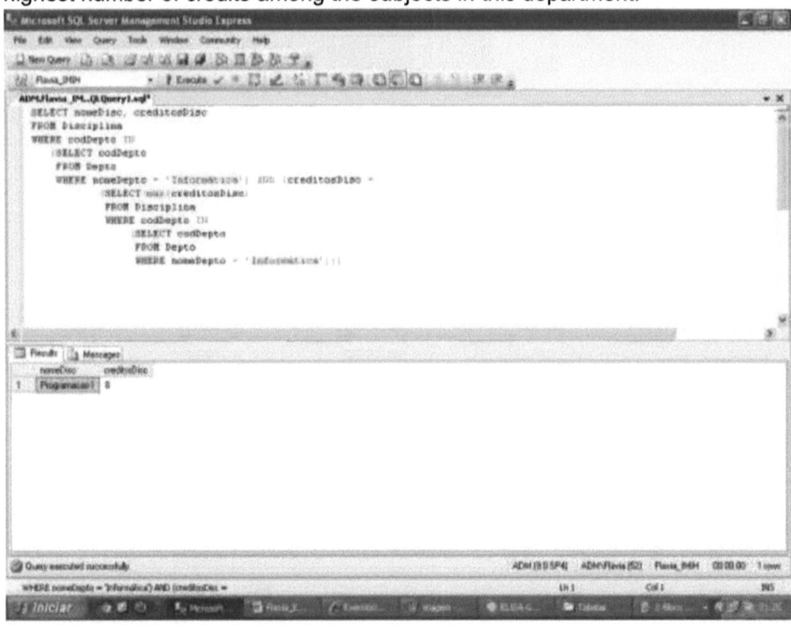

```
ADM.Flavia_IM...QLQuery1.sql*
    SELECT nomeDisc, creditosDisc
    FROM Disciplina
    WHERE codDepto IN
        (SELECT codDepto
        FROM Depto
        WHERE nomeDepto = 'Informática') AND (creditosDisc =
                (SELECT max(creditosDisc)
                FROM Disciplina
                WHERE codDepto IN
                    (SELECT codDepto
                    FROM Depto
                    WHERE nomeDepto = 'Informática')))
```

	nomeDisc	creditosDisc
1	Programacao I	8

16. For each department, get its name and the number of courses in the department. Obtain the result in descending order of number of courses.

	nomedepto	qtdeDisc
1	Informática	3
2	Matemática	2
3	Eletrônica	0

Printed by Books on Demand GmbH, Norderstedt / Germany